moja means one

moja means one

SWAHILI COUNTING BOOK

by Muriel Feelings · pictures by Tom Feelings

PUFFIN BOOKS

Text copyright © 1971 by Muriel Feelings • Illustrations copyright © 1971 by Tom Feelings

All rights reserved • Library of Congress Catalog Card Number: 76-134856

First Pied Piper Printing 1976

Printed in China by WKT

40 39 38 37 36 35

MOJA MEANS ONE is published in a hardcover edition by

Dial Books for Young Readers,

375 Hudson Street, New York, New York 10014

ISBN 0-14-054662-6

To all Black children living
in the Western Hemisphere,
hoping you will one day
speak the language—in Africa

the continent of Africa,
showing countries where
Swahili is spoken

NILE

RIVER

CONGO

ZAIRE

UGANDA
Kampala ★

KENYA

SOMALIA

★ Mogadishu

RWANDA
Bujumbura ★ ★Kigali
BURUNDI

★ Nairobi

+ MT. KILIMANJARO

Brazzaville ★

★ Kinshasa

TANZANIA

★ Dar es Salaam

Z A M B I A

M A L A W

Lusaka ★

★ Zomba

M O Z A M B I Q U E

MALAGASY REPUBLIC

★ Tananarive

★ Lourenço Marques

introduction

All over the world people speak different languages. Languages differ according to the country or society in which people live. People use numbers for counting, and the words for numbers are from the words of their language. You may know some words from languages other than English, but do you know any words from an African language?

Africa, one of the largest continents in the world, spreads over 11 million square miles. There are about 800 African languages spoken in the many nations of this vast continent. Swahili is spoken across a wider geographical area than any other single language. It is the language of about 45 million people in the eastern part of Africa: in Kenya, Uganda, two-fifths of Zaire, on the coasts of Mozambique and Somalia, in the northern part of Malawi and Zambia, and by the townspeople of Rwanda, Burundi, and in Rhodesia as a language of commerce. It is spoken on the islands off the coast of East Africa such as Seychelles, Kilwa, and the Malagasy Republic. It is the national language of Tanzania. A person from Zaire can speak with a person of Kenya, a Tanzanian can talk with a Ugandan or Rwandan. One major importance of learning Swahili is that it serves as a common language and a unifying force among the many varying cultures and countries of Africa.

I lived for two years in Uganda and taught in a high school in Kampala, the capital. I also had the opportunity to travel around Uganda, to parts of Kenya, Tanzania, and Zaire, visiting with families in cities and villages throughout the countryside. Though the people in each country were of various ethnic groups and spoke their own language, they also spoke Swahili. Therefore I could communicate with them, though my knowledge of Swahili was limited. I found that in learning this language, I understood more of the culture (the way of life, the customs, values, history) of my people in East Africa.

Africa is the original homeland of about 100 million Black people who live in the United States, Canada, Central and South America, and the Caribbean islands. As our people in the Western Hemisphere learn more and more about our African heritage, we become increasingly proud. Part of our heritage is language. For example, in various Black communities in the United States, many of our people have taken Swahili names, Black students are learning Swahili in schools and colleges, private schools and shops bear Swahili names such as *Uhuru Sasa* (Freedom Now) School and *Uhuru Kitabu* (Freedom Book) Shop.

I have written this book in the hope that young boys and girls of African origin will enjoy learning to count in Swahili, together with gaining more knowledge of their African heritage.

Muriel Feelings

moja means one

1 moja
(mo·jah)

Snowy Kilimanjaro is the highest mountain in Africa.

mbili
(m·bee·lee)

Mankala, a counting game, is played by villagers young and old.

3 tatu

(ta·too)

Farmers grow **coffee trees** in all parts of East Africa.

4 nne
(n·nay)

Mothers usually carry their babies on their backs while walking.

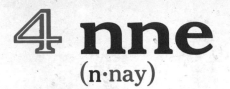

5 tano

(tah·no)

Many kinds of animals roam the grassy savannah lands.

6 sita
(see·tah)

The clothing East Africans wear includes the kanga, busuti, lapa, kanzu, and dashiki.

7 saba
(sah·bah)

The Nile River, which flows between Uganda and Egypt, is filled with fish.

8 nane
(nah·nay)

Busy market stalls are stocked with fruits, vegetables, meats, fish, clothes, jewelry, pottery, and carvings.

⑨ tisa
(tee·sah)

Men play drums, thumb pianos, bamboo flutes, and other instruments.

10 kumi
(koo·mee)

At night in villages old people tell stories to children around the fireside.

Kiswahili is the proper name for the language we call Swahili. The prefix *ki* denotes the actual language rather than the people who speak the language. (For example, a person who speaks Swahili would refer to the language spoken by the Ganda people as "kiganda," and to the Luo language as "kiluo.")

Because city life is basically similar around the world, I have not discussed it in this book. My intent rather has been to acquaint readers with what is unique about East African life. It is important, however, that children also learn about African cities, governments, universities, commerce, the arts, and other aspects of African culture.

MURIEL FEELINGS was born in Philadelphia, Pennsylvania, and attended California State College. She has lived in Guyana, South America, and in East Africa, where she taught for two years. Upon her return to the United States she taught high-school art in Brooklyn, New York. Her book *Jambo Means Hello: Swahili Alphabet Book* (Dial and Puffin Pied Piper), the companion to *Moja Means One*, was also illustrated by Tom Feelings and was a Caldecott Honor Book, an ALA Notable, and a Child Study Association Book of the Year. Ms. Feelings currently lives in Philadelphia.

TOM FEELINGS, well-known illustrator and artist, was born in Brooklyn, New York, and attended the School of Visual Arts. In 1971 Mr. Feelings became the first African-American artist to win a Caldecott Honor with his illustrations for *Moja Means One* (Dial and Puffin Pied Piper). Among the other award-winning books he has illustrated are *To Be a Slave*, a Newbery Honor Book by Julius Lester, and most recently the Coretta Scott King Award winner *Soul Looks Back in Wonder* (both Dial), a celebration of African-American creativity for which such distinguished writers as Maya Angelou, Margaret Walker, and Walter Dean Myers wrote poems. Mr. Feelings is a professor of art at the University of South Carolina in Columbia, South Carolina.

This Faber book belongs to

....

Read the book, sing the song,
watch the film, dance along!
kitchendiscobook.com

VERY BERRY

BANANAS FOR YOU

I ♥ APPLES

YEP

Mmm!

For the beloved Foges fruit –
Mum, Chris, Barley, Harry and Molly
C. F.

To Kim, Dave & Gareth –
my own Kitchen Disco crew
A. M.

'THIS IS **SO FUNNY**, DOES THIS REALLY HAPPEN WHEN I GO TO BED?'
JOSH, AGE 5

First published in the UK in 2015,
and first published in the USA in 2017, by
Faber and Faber Limited, Bloomsbury House,
74–77 Great Russell Street, London WC1B 3DA.
Text copyright © Clare Foges, 2015. Illustration copyright ©
Al Murphy, 2015. ISBN 978-0-571-33697-5 All rights reserved.
Printed in China.
1 3 5 7 9 10 8 6 4 2
The moral rights of Clare Foges and Al Murphy have been
asserted. A CIP record for this book is available
from the British Library.

FABER & FABER
has published children's books since 1929. Some of our very first publications included *Old Possum's Book of Practical Cats* by T. S. Eliot, starring the now world-famous Macavity, and *The Iron Man* by Ted Hughes. Our catalogue at the time said that 'it is by reading such books that children learn the difference between the shoddy and the genuine'. We still believe in the power of reading to transform children's lives.

GREAT STUFF

I ♥ BANANA

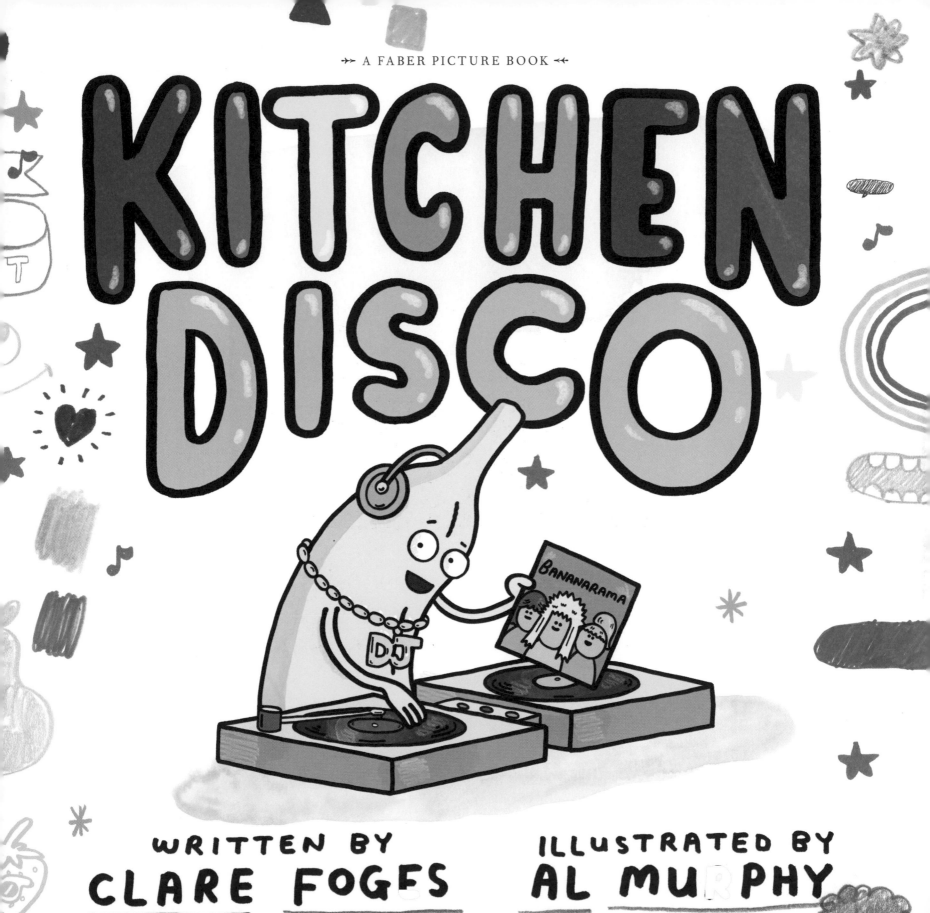

AT NIGHT WHEN YOU ARE SLEEPING THERE'S A PARTY IN YOUR HOUSE.

IT'S A PUMPING, JUMPING, FUNKY BASH
WHEN ALL THE LIGHTS GO OUT...

IN THE QUIET OF YOUR KITCHEN
WHEN THE MOON IS SHINING WHITE

THE FRUIT JUMP FROM THE FRUIT BOWL
AND THEY DANCE ALL THROUGH THE NIGHT!

HE SPINS.

HE JUMPS,

HE
SOMERSAULTS,

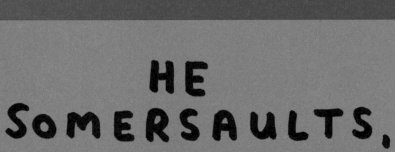

oww!

THEN DOES
BANANA SPLITS.

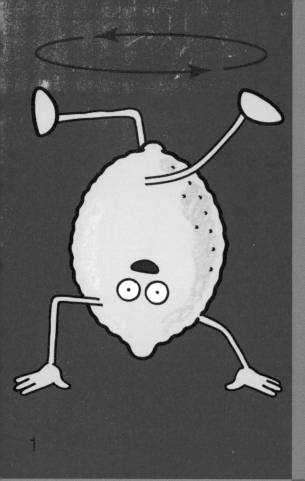

1

2

3

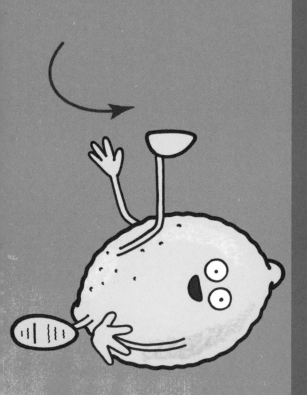

4

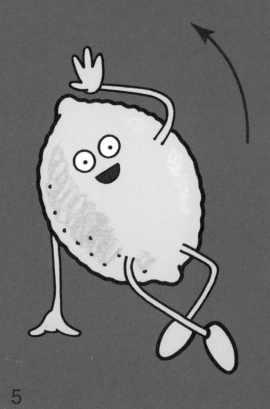

5

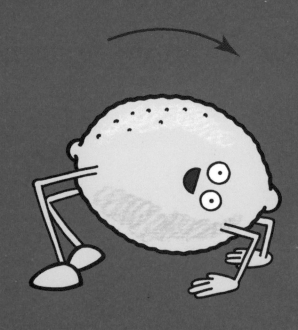

6

THE **LEMONS** ARE
THE SHOW-OFFS
THEY REALLY LOVE TO RAP
THEY BREAK DANCE ON THE
CHOPPING BOARD
AND TAP DANCE ON THE TAP...

THE COCONUT IS CHEEKY, HE MAKES THE OTHERS LAUGH,

HE DIVES INTO THE WASHING-UP... AND HAS A BUBBLE BATH!

ONE TANGERINE SPUN
ROUND SO MUCH
THAT ALL HER JUICE CAME OUT!

THE PINEAPPLE

IS VERY COOL
HE WEARS HIS HAIR IN SPIKES
HE HANGS OUT BY THE MICROWAVE
HIGH-FIVING FRUIT HE LIKES...

BA-DOING!

IT'S CALLED THE KITCHEN DISCO

AND EVERYONE'S INVITED
SO MOVE YOUR HIPS
SHAKE YOUR PIPS
AND LET'S GET ALL EXCITED!

VERY BERRY

THE **GRAPES** ARE SUCH
A SILLY BUNCH, THEY BOOGIE IN A CONGA!
WHEN ALL THE OTHER FRUIT JOIN IN
THE CONGA LINE GETS LONGER!

CONGA!

So shake it like a mango
party like a pear
wiggle like an apple...

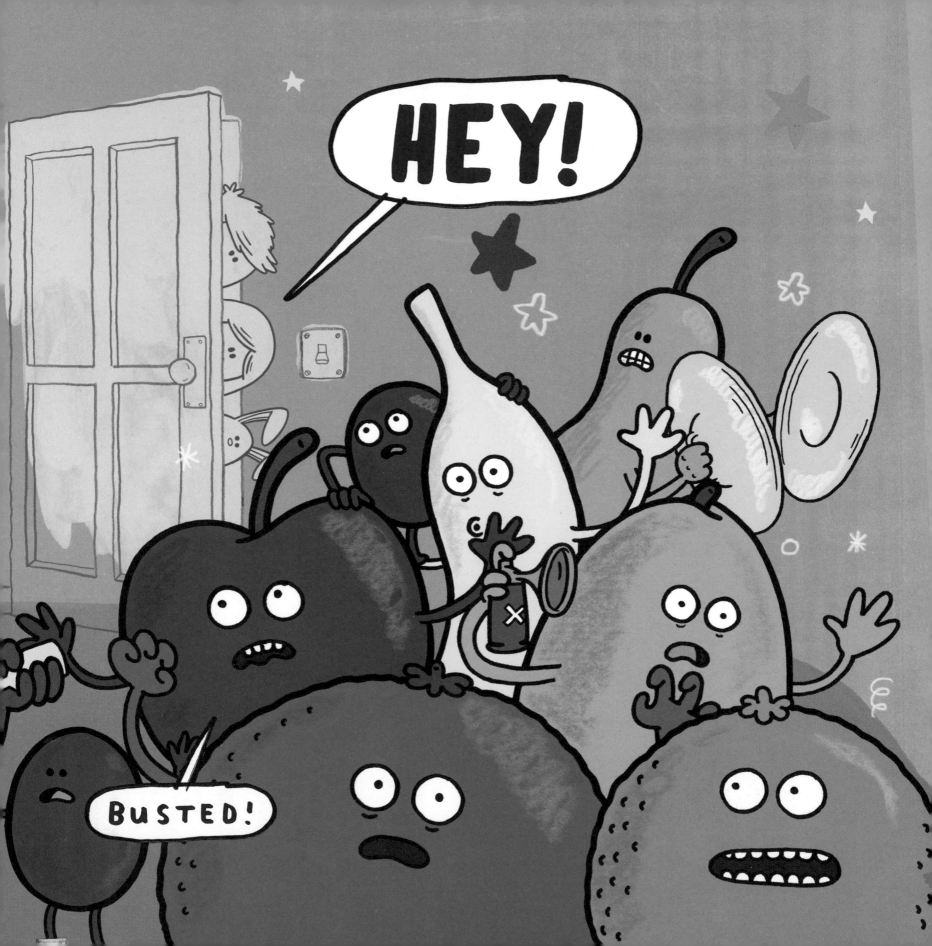

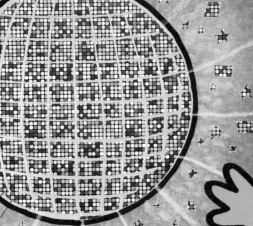

AND **EVERYONE'S** INVITED
SO MOVE YOUR HIPS
SHAKE YOUR PIPS
AND LET'S GET ALL EXCITED!

AT BREAKFAST TIME, THE PARTY SLOWS.
THE FRUIT MUST GO TO BED.

THEY CLIMB IN TO THE FRUIT BOWL...
AND THEY REST THEIR SLEEPY HEADS.

SO IF YOU'RE IN THE KITCHEN
AND YOU HEAR THEM SING THIS SONG
THEN DON'T ASK WHY
AND DON'T BE SHY —
COME ON AND SING ALONG!